Wanted
Employee Thieves

How this Forensic Fraud Examiner
can save you Time, Money and Stress.

John A. Capizzi, CFE, FACFE, DABFE, CHS-3

John A. Capizzi, CFE, FACFE, DABFE, CHS-3

Disclaimer

The information provided herein should be used only as a guide and not as the only source of reference.

The author and firm will have neither liability nor responsibility to any person or entity with respect to any loss, damage or injury caused or alleged to be caused directly or indirectly by any information contained in or admitted from this publication.

DEDICATION

This book is dedicated to my parents Mary and Alfred Capizzi
who have been there for me in all of my trials and tribulations and who
have sacrificed to give me every opportunity to succeed.
Thank you and I love you.

John A. Capizzi, CFE, FACFE, DABFE, CHS-3

CONTENTS

CONTENTS

Continued on next page

CONTENTS

ACKNOWLEDGMENTS

I would like to thank my instructors, foreign and domestic, in the art of Interview and Interrogation. You know who you are.

Jeff Koch, CPA and mentor, who when I first met him, told me "I couldn't afford him but that he has seen entrepreneurs come in and out of his office and that my idea would be a success."

Donna Elmini- Jacobs, my right hand, good friend and IAS secretary that makes me sound and look professional and who puts up with me.

Walter Kasparack, who was with me when we created the IAS logo on the back of a napkin

Al Langston, for his friendship and always words of encouragement

Friends, professionals, attorneys who trusted me and my skills with their reputations and their firm's clients, namely (alphabetically):

Lisa Berg, Esq., Partner, Stearns, Weaver, Miller, Weissler, Alhadeff & Sitterson;

Charles Caulkins, Esq., Managing Partner, Fisher and Phillips;

Diane Geller, Esq., Partner, Fox Rothschild LLP;

ACKNOWLEDGMENTS

Mark Skipper, Esq., Principal, Skipper Law Group;

Don Works, Esq., Partner, Jackson Lewis P.C.

To all my clients over the years that have trusted me with their companies confidential matters.

Dennis D'Andrea, and the boys of the network group, On Target, for their friendship, support and ideas for the title, *Wanted: Employee Thieves.*

Lee Salinas for her efforts in the initiation of this book.

Sal Trovato and his team at 701 Creative for reformatting and creative input.

* If I left anyone out, it is by sheer accident and not due to my lack of gratitude.*

If you are one of those people, I apologize and thank you for all your support.

John A. Capizzi, CFE, FACFE, DABFE, CHS-3

TESTIMONIALS

I have served a plethora of industries through IAS services.
They include but are not limited to:

- Accounting
- Aerospace
- Automotive
- Brokers/Consultants
- Building Services Contracting
- Communications
- Contracting, Construction, and Supply
- Education
- Financial
- Food Services
- Freight Forwarding and Logistics
- Hospitality
- Hotels/Resorts
- Human Resource Consultants
- Industrial
- Insurance
- Legal
- Medical
- Professional Sports
- Security and Alarm

TESTIMONIALS

In the next few pages you will find a small summary of highlights from recommendations and thank you letters that I have received over the years. Keep in mind these are only the highlights and even the full recommendation letters found on the IAS web site are not an exhaustive list of satisfied clients:

Some have passed on, some have moved on to other positions and many are still running and growing their businesses. However, all my clients have become friends to a degree. Now with years plus since some testimonials were gathered, I want to include their names in this book as a way of saying thank you for their confidence in me.

Many a friend, client and lecture attendee have told me repeatedly that they love hearing my "Stories" and "you should write a book."

Well, here you go.

Many who have attended my presentations or I have worked with on cases know that I teach by case example, so you will find this book laced with my teaching examples and case "Stories."

TESTIMONIALS

"I have had the pleasure of working alongside John for two decades as a C level executive of three international companies. I learn from John each time we talk and his counsel is always sound. His unconventional approaches to clever schemes keep him one step ahead of the bad guys who work amongst us. He is the definition of a professional skeptic".

- Paul Donahue, Centerra Group CEO/ Constellis COO; Formerly G4S GS President & CEO; WSI, COO and CFO

"I have known John Capizzi for over 9 years. He helped me resolve a very unpleasant business situation resulting in a successful resolution. I highly recommend John as an outstanding and professional Forensic Fraud Examiner."

- Joseph Ehrenreich, President, Auto Show, Inc. Phila, PA

"John Capizzi is a dedicated professional and committed to provide proven results. He is dogged, tenacious, affable and sincere. John always delivers the goods."

- Frank Giordano, Philly Pops, CEO ; The Union League of Philadelphia Past President.

"We had a fraud issue at the company and had identified the culprit but could not readily determine the extent of the issue and potential involvement of other parties. John was instrumental in helping us not only elucidate the scope and extent of the issue but also extracted a full confession and testimonial from the suspect. John's thorough questioning, attention to detail, and keen sense of truth or lies are key attributes to the successful outcome he generated. It also helped us improve our internal controls."

- Bruce Learner, CEO Peroxy Chem, Philadelphia, Pa.

"John worked closely with our executive management and internal auditors professionally resolving and minimizing problems for our business. He is relentless in protecting his client's interests and a very valuable asset to any company needing to pro-actively resolve and prevent internal problems."

- Muna Issa, Managing Director, Super Clubs Resorts, Kingston, Jamaica

TESTIMONIALS

"John Capizzi is a true professional who never hesitated to assist me, taking my numerous phone calls and responding to many emails during off hours and during the weekend and very inconvenient times for most people, but not for John. He assisted me personally and my company (IFS) through a very difficult time with an employee embezzlement issue. If not for John's efforts, as he was successful in coordinating a full confession from the embezzler, we would not have been able to prosecute the embezzler to the full extent of the law and realize some satisfaction and retribution. The embezzler was sentenced to a minimum nine months of jail time and to required financial restitution. None of this would have been possible without John's efforts. If you don't hire John to assist with a fraud, theft, embezzlement or related issue, you are working with the second team. Make sure you use the first team and don't take any chances... he is worth it!!"
- **Michael D. Ryan, President and CEO, Innovative Financing Solutions (IFS) Ardmore, Pa.**

"I have known John Capizzi for approximately 28 years. He is innovative and extremely detailed with his unique approach to problem solving."
- **Koch Reiss & Company, P.A., Jeffrey B. Koch, CPA/PFS**

"In the 20+ years that I have worked with John Capizzi, he has achieved remarkable success for my clients. He's extremely intelligent, ethical, diligent, responsive, and a true expert in his field. Over the years, he has managed to obtain signed, lawful confessions from dozens of employees, as well as, restitution agreements resulting in the return of thousands of dollars in stolen money. Not only does John identify the sources of losses, he helps his clients implement measures to prevent similar incidents from occurring in the future. If you're looking for results, look no further.. John Capizzi is the real deal."
- **Lisa Berg, Esq. Partner Stearns, Weaver, Miller, Weissler, Alhadeff & Sitterson, P.A.**

TESTIMONIALS

"I've worked with John Capizzi and Internal Audit Services for over 27 years. In this regard, I have referred many of my clients who have suspected internal theft and related issues to IAS. John and team are responsive and thorough. In many cases, John has been able to obtain the conclusive evidence along with confessions that resolve the matter. I highly recommend John and team to any company needing a Forensic Fraud Examination and Loss Prevention auditing services."

- Charles Caulkins, Esq., Managing Partner, Fisher and Phillips

"John has delivered a successful investigation every time I have recommended him to my clients including confessions, a roadmap of how the fraud was committed and recommendations for future avoidance. He has also been invaluable in assisting clients detect and close loopholes that help avoid losses from occurring."

- Diane Geller, Esq., Partner, Fox Rothschild, LLP

"I've known John Capizzi for over 30 years. In the times we worked together, I always found him to be professional and to have expertise in internal audit matters. I referred him to clients and they've always been pleased with the results obtained."

- Don Works, Esq., Principal, Jackson Lewis P. C.

"John is truly a dynamic and consummate professional. His investigative services help companies identify, stop and reduce internal fraud, insider abuse and criminal misconduct. John can help by thoroughly investigating the circumstances where fraud may exist to help companies detect it. He can help put an end to insider abuse and can provide a quick resolve in many instances by obtaining written confessions from perpetrators."

- Bill Shipp, Managing Partner, Vaxient-Cybersecurity,
Privacy & Compliance Services Philadelphia, Pa; NY, NY.

TESTIMONIALS

"I met Mr. John Capizzi over 30 years ago and retained his services for the purposes of assisting me in a case in which I represented a local businessman on a charge of Capital Sexual Battery. I asked John to interview my client for the purpose of obtaining necessary information to be used in formulating a defense. I was aware that John had in depth training and experience in interrogation techniques and case analysis; however, I was amazed with what developed due to John's participation in this, as in many other cases.

John had attained a detailed confession, which law enforcement and I had previously been unable to obtain. Preparation of a defense based upon inaccurate facts would have been devastating and exposed me to potential ethical violations.

John has an uncanny talent to ferret-out the truth and is tenacious and relentless in his efforts to protect his client's interest. He possesses unquestionable integrity and professionalism and can be trusted to protect his client's confidentiality in all respects. He is a brilliant investigator, risk analyst and a totally focused problem solver.

John would be an outstanding asset to any potential client. The costs, aggravation and exposure to risk preempted by Mr. Capizzi's services always more than justified his fees."
- **Mark Skipper, Esq. PA Principal Skipper Law Group**

"He maintains the highest standards within his profession and is a valuable business resource to any company."
- **Jeffrey A. Bolton, CPA, Partner, Dazkill, Bolton CPA's**

"Our Firm has worked with John Capizzi for several years… have never been disappointed with the results… clients frequently ask for return speaking engagements by John."
- **Bill Mahoney, Mahoney and Associates**

TESTIMONIALS

"I would not have believed it, unless I saw it for myself…the removal of these employees had a positive effect within our organization and set a precedent for the remainder of the staff. To date, everyone's performance has increased and the employee's attitudes have never been better."
- **Robert M. Fitzgerald; President, Cel-Tec Communications Corp**

"John Capizzi provides a well-organized approach to the investigatory process…from the compilation of evidence through to the successful interview of suspects…true professionalism and integrity in all of the work performed…"
- **Christopher A. Holler, Vice President, Holler Automotive Group**

"John is a tenacious and driven individual that gets his man! John paid off for me tenfold and got me the satisfaction I was looking for when victimized. When your employees think they are smarter than you, John is who you want to show them who knows better."
- **Ted Bohne, Business Consultant**

"Dealing with situations such as fraud and internal theft are never pleasant experiences. The "silver lining in the cloud" of these unfortunate incidents has been the professionalism and personal attention John Capizzi has rendered…we were pleased to be able to bring closure to each, recover a significant amount of loss and be presented with the option to prosecute in a confident manner."
- **Scott Whiddon, President, Causeway Lumber Company**

"I have known John for over 10 years and during that time I have utilized his audit services several times at one of my former companies to address very serious legal issues related to non-compete violations and internal theft. In each case, John and his team did an excellent job gathering very damaging evidence which supported our legal case. Thanks to John's expertise, we were successful in winning each of these cases. I have also referred John to several other companies where they experienced similar success. He is a true professional and an expert in his field."
- **Lawrence Kraska, President and CEO Interim HealthCare, Inc.**

TESTIMONIALS

"While President of MJP Club Management, a national nightclub organization consisting of 24 locations, ranging from Hawaii to New York, Internal Audit Services, specifically, Mr. John Capizzi was engaged to develop, maintain and follow up on all fraud, loss control and all other activities that could otherwise jeopardize the profitable operations of the locations and enjoyment of our patrons… results beyond our expectation resolving loss control issues in a proactive manner. I would highly recommend Internal Audit Services, Inc., International and John Capizzi for any engagement that your company may face."

- Renato Carretin, President, Powermix Productions, Inc.

"…he has great character, expertise, and vast experience in his chosen field of endeavor…"

- Robert D. Helmholdt, D.D.S., P.A.

"John Capizzi and Internal Audit Services bring the highest standards of excellence and expertise to his profession. I highly recommend John and his company for anyone in need of his services."

- Steve Palmer, Vice President; Stiles Corporation

"John has been teaching internal audit procedures to our contractor members since 1998… Any employer who has even the slightest suspicion of theft from an employee should call John. With his experience and expertise he can save a company thousands of dollars by stopping and preventing theft that have caused many businesses to go bankrupt."

- Mike Hadley, United Service Training Corp.,
   Plumbing Workforce of America

"I highly recommend John Capizzi as an outstanding fraud investigator. John is the "real deal" - a true professional."

- Byron C. Russell/ Chairman & C.E.O. Cheney Brothers, Inc. (CBI)

TESTIMONIALS

"…his presence and interviewing of the employees was a big factor in the theft coming to a halt. John also assisted us in implementing a security system for our building that has been beneficial to us in several ways."
- Brad Weinbrum, Chief Operation Officer, ABB Optical

"Thank you for conducting the very professional & successful internal audit for our company."
- Hank Norwell, President, Paul's Abbey Carpet Co.

"…find him to be highly reputable and honest in his dealings with all people. John is the epitome of good service and confidentiality."
- Jean G. Smith, Senior Executive, Vice President SunTrust Bank

"The work I have seen done by Internal Audit Services has been first rate, on the mark and timely… without fear of problems arising after the fact. In the era of … legislation that requires complete disclosure it is a comfort to know that Internal Audit Services has gone over the numbers in their usual highly professional and thorough manner."
- John D. Gullman, Principal; GSR Partners

"I would highly recommend John Capizzi and his company (Internal Audit Services, Inc.) for any corporate fraud investigations. At our Bank, John was able to solve an employee embezzlement using his behavior analysis interviewing techniques… constantly shown true professionalism and integrity…"
**- James J. Sutter, CPA, Internal Auditor of the City Miami Beach
(Former Director of Internal Audit – Jefferson National Bank)**

John performed an operational audit for our practice during a time of transition… the results of this audit provided tremendous insight into existing problems and ways to improve our day to day operations while decreasing stress for our doctors and staff."
- Dr. Anthony Sclar, South Florida OMS, Partner

TESTIMONIALS

"John Capizzi takes an aggressive approach to determining the various suspects in a theft and recommends various ways to tighten security and procedures to prevent future mishaps."
- Patricia A. Stanford SPHR, Human Resources Director, Hellmann Worldwide Logistics, Inc.

"...GPS Logistics' multi-state engagement with Internal Audit Services was handled in a prompt and professional manner bringing about quick closure to unpleasant matters which enabled us to get back to business and allowed us the choice of prosecution and or restitution through signed confessions."
- Michael Collins, Vice President Operations, Yellow GPS Logistics

"John Capizzi is a great person professionally and personally. John has provided outstanding service and 100% efficiency."
-Jay Brown, President, Too Jays Deli

"John Capizzi has been very helpful...He presented a seminar that gave us great insight as to how he could help us control our theft at our company."
- Walter Banks, President, Lago Mar Resort

"...every now and then we all come across some rotten apples which can spoil the trust that you have placed on most of your workers...At a moment of pure desperation to find the culprits of missing cargo, I phoned John Capizzi...I must say that John has a very unique and effective way of going through an elimination process to find the guilty parties. This allowed me to restore my faith in my staff and maintain our commitment to our customers of a Theft Free Warehouse."
- Mary Prado, Miami Branch Manager, Salviati and Santura/Centerport

TESTIMONIALS

"...excellent reputation and high client satisfaction... he continually gets rave reviews for both his group presentations and his professional services..."
- **Thomas H. Shea, CEO & Managing Principal, Right Management Consultants**

"We had an unfortunate theft incident and needed immediate resolution... All employees were treated with dignity and respect."
- **John Trost, General Manager, Cintas Corporation**

"John Capizzi provides truly outstanding fraud investigative services. He is meticulous in his preparation and due diligence with a genuine commitment to only doing things right! Importantly, he displays a heartfelt compassion towards his clients during some challenging and humbling situations. These qualities, in a very real sense, enable Mr. Capizzi to help take the sting out of getting stung."
- **Dr. Peter Sarbone, M.D. Physician-Dermatologist**

"...willing and expert speaker at our events. Each time you spoke, your presentations were always well attended and received... certainly grateful for your continued service to the university and students... you have taken the time to provide career counseling in forensics to students... demonstrates selfless dedication to your profession and community. Thank you."
- **Alan H. Friedberg, Professor of Accounting, Florida Atlantic University**

"I have known John Capizzi for many years as a member of the Executive Association of Ft. Lauderdale... very high praise for his professionalism and his knowledge..."
- **Nathan A. Goren, Director Community Affairs,**
  North Broward Hospital District

TESTIMONIALS

"Having been in the security industry for over 13 years, I have personally been involved with clients who have experienced losses to their company, both to external (customers, vendors, etc.) and internal (employee) factors. These losses have on many occasions been very large, and quite frequently, extremely damaging to the organization.

Internal Audit Services, Inc., and John Capizzi, have, in our opinion, proven themselves as exceptionally talented in identifying the source of losses to a company, and in implementing procedures and policies to prevent the events from reoccurring."

- John Ray, III, President, Sonitrol of Ft. Lauderdale

"I've known John professionally for over 28 years. I heard all the stories about his work. I didn't really understand the power or believe the entire story until I needed his services and he told me that when he was done we would have a signed confession, a resignation and restitution from the thief. I laughed, not thinking it was possible. Only two hours into the interview, John emerged, with a smile on his face and said, "I've got a signed confession, a resignation and restitution"... Thanks John."

- Ron Santini, CPA, PFS (from back cover)

FOREWORD

Each year, over $900 billion is stolen from businesses by employees. These employee-thieves might not think their fraudulent actions have a significant impact on their employer or weaken the financial and competitive strength of the company, but it all adds up. Theft can never be justified.

In his book, "Wanted: Employee Thieves," John Capizzi, founder and CEO of Internal Audit Services, Inc., Int'l., outlines his approach to getting employees to confess to their theft and wrongdoing. Part detective, part psychologist, and low-key interrogator, he is able to win the trust of employees who might not be expected to admit to fraud.

Reading about his approach to building rapport with the suspected employee, one would think that confessing fraudulent actions to Capizzi would be much less traumatic than facing a police detective who may not be so skilled in Capizzi's approach.

Capizzi has developed his approach over many years practicing his craft and studying the best practices of effective interrogators. The entire encounter with the suspect is choreographed, from the initial encounter to the discussion which convinces the employee that the best course of action is to confess to Capizzi and pay restitution. The alternative is to face the criminal justice system including the cost of defense attorneys. There is a high risk that the fraud could go public resulting in embarrassment to the company and personal embarrassment for the individual employee and his or her family.

In many cases, restitution is all that is wanted by companies, not criminal charges brought against the individual. When faced with the alternatives, Capizzi gets his confession.

His client's get cost effective peace of mind knowing that a costly internal problem has been removed after the fact, or preventive measures have been established and proactively infused into the workforce preventing and/or minimizing future internal problems whereby increasing the financial and competitive strength of the company.

Stanley W. Silverman
Nationally syndicated writer on Leadership,
Entrepreneurship and Corporate Governance,
Former President & CEO of PQ Corporation,
Vice Chairman, Drexel University,
Founder & CEO, Silverman Leadership

John A. Capizzi, CFE, FACFE, DABFE, CHS-3

"I should have had a statement, I locked up a bank employee and her husband for stealing $100K out of a customer's account. The bank refused to pay until she was arrested."

Detective Steven Parkinson, Central Detectives, Philadelphia Police Department

1. INTERNAL AUDIT SERVICES (IAS)

IAS Mission Statement:

IAS strives to provide a proactive no hassle solution to Internal Fraud and Employment Practices Liability (EPL) situations. From large corporations to three seat hair salons, no business is too large or too small.

Fraud hurts everyone, from the companies that take the financial hit, to the communities that receive less due to the loss, to the guilty employees and their families that suffer under the weight of the fraud.

Exposing the fraud and liability not only saves the company money, allowing it to provide more for its employees and community by spending less on investigating the loss; but it also helps the guilty individual by releasing the burden of covering up the fraud so they can face their wrongs and make it right.

However, taking legal action with police investigators or lawyers is messy, time-consuming, stressful and expensive. The IAS proactive approach is both successful and cost effective.

Who is Internal Audit Services?

Throughout the following chapters you will come to know me, my approach and how I created the IAS process.

When I founded Internal Audit Services (IAS) in 1989 my thought was to develop a company that would bring Corporate Loss Prevention and internal audit skills in the investigation of Fraud, as well as, Employment Practices Liability and Physical Vulnerability Assessments to companies that do not have Corporate Loss Prevention or Internal Auditors.

For example, the dry cleaner in the mall, the mom-and-pop restaurant on the corner, the bar around the block etc... Over the years, my clientele has ranged from aerospace companies, pro sports teams, fast food chains, down to a three chair ladies' hairdresser salon.

IAS was formed to prevent fraud and internal theft from occurring in a company and if it did occur to identify all involved in the activity.

One might ask why such a diversified clientele? The reason being is because the original premise of my company was to serve small mom-and-pop operations that do not have Loss Prevention or Internal Audit and while still doing so now, it allows for ongoing practice in conducting forensic interviews as well as maintaining a marketing presence within the community.

For example:

Several years ago, I had a wine rack installed in my South Florida home. About a year later I received a call from the installer saying: "I remember you telling me what you did. I'm hoping you can help me or tell me where I can find help. My wife Cathy owns a beauty salon and rented a chair to another hairdresser and she thinks she is stealing." I responded saying, that's exactly what I handle and I can help her.

Our suspect hairdresser was a recently divorced single parent, whose plan was to open her own hair cutting practice and go into business for herself.

To do this she stole supplies identified as shampoos, dyes, scissors (valued at $200 to $300 per instrument), cash payments and the biggest commodity – the salon clients. She would tell clients that "you're paying this $$$ here, I will go to your house or office and cut your hair for less."

In just one hour I was able to obtain a signed confession, restitution for items stolen and an injunction preventing the suspect from cutting hair within a specific geographic distance from Cathy's beauty salon. The injunction took a little longer to accomplish but Cathy's problem was solved.

What is IAS?

My company name Internal Audit Services can be somewhat misleading. Let me say it, the name Stinks! When you hear the name Internal Audit Services typically one thinks my company is the IRS or a tax accounting firm. I chose the name primarily for presentation to the dishonest or questionable employee for (Effect) and not so much for introduction to potential clients.

The reason being, I need to be effective in obtaining a confession for clients in order for them to remain clients, or for me to be referred to new clients.

Frankly, I would love my company name to be Capizzi and Associates, however if I said to a dishonest employee: I am John from Capizzi and Associates the employee would look at me and say, "Who Cares!" Whereas, when I identify myself to a dishonest employee and introduce myself as John, Lead Internal Auditor, Internal Audit, I immediately have their attention. From the time I step foot on a client's property, all actions are choreographed with the idea that the dishonest employee or employees are watching and listening to see if anyone is on their trail.

Let me explain what I mean by choreographed:

Once a room is determined to conduct the interviews in, (room setting will be discussed in a later chapter) I will then tell the owner of the company or highest ranking management official to go bring me the interviewee. Typically, the response is "how do I get them there?" My reply is simple, you're the owner just say to them follow me.

When you (or your designee) arrive at the interview room you will find the door ajar, knock and enter. I will then take it from there by introducing myself to the interviewee, directing them where to sit so as to prevent false imprisonment allegations. Then I will turn to you and say, we are not to be disturbed, if any auditors or anyone else calls just take a message. Your pre-instructed reply will be, "Yes Sir," then leave and close the door.

This strategy quickly gets the employees attention leaving them asking themselves, who is this guy in the suit and tie that just basically told the owner of the company or ranking management to take a memo and the boss's reply was, "Yes Sir."

This attention getter coupled with my introduction as Lead Internal Auditor quickly has the employee focused. It is further alluded that my presence at the company is due to the financial or insurance entities backing the company, looking into causes of loss, risk and liability, breach of policy and procedures and not due to the owner or management sending me there just to question employees.

Example:

During a recent case, I was assisted by a senior accounting management employee. I intentionally kept calling him by the wrong name. The suspect employees interviewed believed that I was from outside banking/ insurance entities auditing the company for causes of loss, risk and liability deflecting my presence from association with company management.

To better appreciate the emotion that these techniques/strategies create, consider this scenario.

Example:

It's Friday night and you're on your way home from a night out on the town. You're two blocks from your house and find yourself stopped at a traffic light. Nobody is on the road and you suddenly get the idea that if I run this light I can be home in two minutes.

You look to your left, you look to your right, you look behind you; doing this exercise several times, all along your heart is pounding. You may start to sweat and your heart is pumping faster. Your anxiety is building while you are trying to work up the courage to hit the gas and run the red traffic light. You repeat this process again but this time you get the nerve and now you hit the gas and run the light!

What are you doing for the next two blocks?? That's right, you're looking in the rearview mirror for blue lights and the police!! Now, all you did is knowingly break a traffic law by running the red light and nobody is around to witness it.

Imagine the anxiety that a dishonest employee is feeling when brought to an office or conference room by the company owner or executive management then introduced to the "Lead Auditor" and the employee knowingly stole intellectual property (cyber information); cash; inventory or violated company policies and procedures or has knowledge of friends, coworkers and peers doing the same.

IAS Arsenal

Combatting Suspicious and Dishonest Employees:

In a Forensic Interview, I do most of the talking for about 30-40 minutes while walking the suspect down a psychological trail identifying what I do, how we do it, how they were identified, why they did what they did, and the emotions they are feeling while I am talking to them. At the end of that 30-40 minutes, they have one move to make.

The move is to make a conscious decision to lie or make a conscious decision to tell the truth.

The arsenal I utilize in identifying the wrongdoer in your business whether it be the theft of cash, inventory, intellectual property, leakage of information, breach of policy and procedures or Employment Practices Liability (EPL), etc. is:

The direct Forensic Interview - used when I have a finite number of interviewees - and an Israeli technique - when I have a large number of interviewees and unknown suspects of who did what. An added benefit to using this technique is that it: eliminates unnecessary interviews and costs; allows employees to identify how the situation developed in the first place from their perspective; allows informants to step forward; and provides a blue print to develop a corrective action plan so the situation doesn't happen again.

The following page has a list of questions and areas of concern for you to consider.

Questions and Areas of Concern that will be discussed in the following chapters will assist me/IAS in helping and assisting you, and in you helping me help you, when dealing with potential internal wrongdoing and allegations of wrongdoing in your company:

1) Who notified you to the allegations of internal wrongdoing;
2) Did you identify the potential problem yourself;
3) When and how were you notified;
4) What evidence has been gathered;
5) Was anybody interviewed;
6) If yes, by whom;
7) What questions were asked;
8) What was the immediate and exact response to the questions when asked;
9) Outside of you and/or the initial person that notified you - who else is aware of the incident or allegations;
10) When to call police and when not to;
11) When to notify your insurance company in regards to crime coverage;
12) Has any attorney been retained;
13) Have you given any statement, verbal or written;
14) Developing your probable cause typed/written statement, necessary for the development of the fraud examination, police involvement, insurance claim.

The reason for these questions and examples are spelled out in the chapters ahead. For your convenience, after each chapter I have included a short summary and a page for you to take notes on any "ah's", concerns or questions you may have for me when you call.

<u>Summary of Key Points:</u>

- ✔ IAS mission, how we fit in with the community, and what inspires our mission.
  - Fraud hurts everyone, person, company and community

- ✔ What we do
  - Bringing Corporate Loss Prevention and internal audit skills to companies that do not have it

- ✔ Who we help
  - Large corporations to three-seat hair salons, no business too large or too small.

- ✔ Why we started
  - To serve small mom-and-pop operations that do not have Loss Prevention or Internal Audit

- ✔ A peek into the IAS arsenal
  - The Forensic Interview

- ✔ Key questions and concerns to consider while reading this book
  - 14 major questions to keep in mind

Notes or Questions for John

Does the IAS mission reach you?

Wanted: Employee Thieves

"I didn't really understand the power or believe the entire story until I needed his services.. He told me that when he was done we would have a signed confession, a resignation and restitution from the thief."

Ron Santini, CPA, PFS

2. FORENSIC FRAUD EXAMINER?

What is a Forensic Accountant vs a Forensic Fraud Examiner:

People, friends, clients and potential clients initially confuse me with a Forensic Accountant and sometimes a Private Investigator. <u>I am emphatically neither.</u>

It drives me crazy!

So what's the difference between a Forensic Accountant and a Forensic Fraud Examiner?

Well, let's start by defining Forensic. Forensic simply means: for court. The Forensic Accountant will do the accounting, collecting sufficient data to support the opinion rendered, then testify in court about his accounting findings or lack of accounting findings. Credentials typically require a Bachelor's Degree in accounting or business and preferably also hold a CPA certification.

The Forensic Fraud Examiner imparts forensic methods, law, and techniques to resolve specific allegations of fraud including determining if fraud occurred, who is responsible, conducting interviews, gathering evidence to support or refute an allegation of fraud and testifying to such.

Credential requirements include:

• A Bachelor's Degree, from an accredited college or university in any field but preferred business, accounting, law, psychology,

• A stipulated minimum fraud investigative experience (obtained from law enforcement, military, corporate loss prevention) to qualify to sit for the CFE, Certified Fraud Examiner Certification Exam,

• Pass the exam encompassing law both criminal and civil, ethics, criminology, accounting then maintain CPE credits.

• For Forensic Board certification, additional testing, board review and more CPE.

• IAS further requires advanced training and experience in interview and interrogation techniques and skills.

I don't do Private Investigator work such as surveillance, background investigations, chasing down cheating husbands and wives, etc., etc., etc...I will however, outsource and provide you with a reputable referral, through IAS's vast contact network, for your private investigator needs.

The IAS Process:

The IAS process is to convey in a proactive non-disruptive manner to a client's employees. Simply put:

- ✔ If you are thinking of stealing, Don't.
- ✔ If you are stealing, Stop.
- ✔ If you continue, you will be identified culminating with a signed confession.

From a Loss Prevention perspective, to illustrate, say you have four employees, if two that were thinking of stealing don't do it, (IT being anything under investigation) that's half your potential loss. If one of the two that are stealing stops, by virtue of my process, that's ¾ of your loss prevention.

You will always have someone doing something, but that will change and be halted or minimized by the creation of controls, loss prevention training, the direct interviews of management and staff, and the conversion of employee's in their beliefs that they are considered valued assets to your company.

My process is structured to proactively clear suspected dishonest employees (if they can be cleared) while making or enhancing their belief that they are a valued asset to your company.

Story Time:

On one occasion, I had to interview a suspect employee who worked third shift, weekends only, on a loading dock. As far as he was concerned, he didn't exist, no one at the company knew who he was, what he did or really cared.

After his shift, he was brought to the designated interview room where I cleared him from being involved with the thefts. The employee left the interview room following his interview a newly energized employee, feeling he was a valued asset to the company with his feelings and company knowledge, and that his operational insight was greatly appreciated and important to the company.

Little did he know that when he entered the office for his interview, he was a suspect!

On another case, my client did not want to prosecute or fire the identified and admitted dishonest employee.

Note: (I personally don't care what my clients want to do with admitted wrongdoers - prosecute, fire, obtain restitution or do nothing.) As a business owner/fraud examiner, its job security for me if you do nothing. The phone will ring again and I'll be back! Sorry, for the fraud examiner sense of humor. Hope you're smiling!

To continue with the case story: The employee admitted to stealing a petty amount of cash and office supplies. However, he was a top salesman, longtime employee and a man that brought in over $100,000 in sales the previous year.

Due to my proactive approach and choreographed presentation to the interviewee the owner was able to "tune up" his employee for lack of verbiage. The owner told the employee that "all he had to do was ask and it would have been given to him." (It being the stolen money and office supplies.)

He went on to say that: "The lead auditor was going to terminate him and prosecute him." The owner told his employee that he "badgered that auditor (Me) all morning until the auditor told him to handle the situation." While holding the employee's confession in his hand and telling the employee how "very disappointed" he was with his long time, trusted employee and friend that had even been to his home, he wasn't going to fire, prosecute or even ask for restitution. The situation would remain between them and his signed confession would be placed in his file.

The employee was in tears promising the world to his employer. The last I heard from my client, his employee was working like a machine and bringing in sale after sale, projecting to double his previous year's sales total.

<u>Why People Confess:</u>

My biggest and constant obstacle to my business is getting clients to believe that I will obtain a written out and signed confession by the dishonest or suspect employee.

Now at this point you are probably saying why would anyone confess let alone put it in writing?!

Let me try to explain this.

First of all, your employees are not master criminals. They are basically honest people that came to your business for one of two reasons and in some cases both reasons.

1) it's what they studied for in school and

2) it's simply a better job than what they had a week ago.

They did not look at your company as an easy place to steal from or wreak havoc on.

Something caused them to do what they did, - opportunity; financial stress; friend; family; peer asked them to do something. For example, a classmate comes in and asks for a free bag of fries. A bartender gives a beer away allegedly to "promote the business" but in reality to promote himself for a better tip out, etc., etc.....

People confess because all honest people are basically all raised the same. Male/female, nationality, race, we are all raised the same-TO BE HONEST.

For example:

My readers with kids, when you catch your child doing something wrong, are they more in trouble for what you caught them doing wrong or for lying to you about what they did wrong? I would bet the answer is, lying to you. This is why they confess. Their upbringing. Street thug to blue collar and white collar worker, basically honest people, are all raised the same.

Story Time:

When two people initially meet, the conversation usually goes something like: what's your name, where are you from, and what do you do?

I was on a flight from Ft. Lauderdale, Florida to Houston, Texas. On this flight I was sitting next to a doctor who basically laughed at me when I told him I was a *Forensic Fraud Examiner and I get confessions from dishonest employees.* His reaction was typical:

What?! That's crazy!, I would never tell you anything!!
I get this reaction all the time…Initially!!

Now given the premise that people like to talk about themselves, all the time, I asked the good doctor what he did. He went on to tell me that he was a practicing physician at an area Houston Medical Center for approximately 10 years. He continued to identify his area of medical specialty and the pros and cons of his specialty. Since he already knew what I did to some degree, I turned the conversation to inquire about theft at the Medical Center.

The doctor went on to identify rampant theft and I asked what type of theft and by whom? The doctor described theft of scrubs, medicines, office supplies etc. I then asked who was doing the thefts? He answered doctors and nurses.

I asked if he ever had taken anything from the Medical Center? The doctor laughingly said, "Yes" and identified scrubs, medicines and other things. I asked him if he knew that was stealing and he said "Yes." I then asked if the Medical Center was to ask for repayment would he repay what he took and he replied, "Of course!"

I went on to ask what shift had the most theft occurrence at the hospital. The doctor replied third shift. I asked why the third shift and he responded by saying because nobody is around and typically security is sleeping.

I then said come on Doc, is that the truth and he replied, "Yes it's the truth!" We had additional small talk and then the good doctor said he was going to take a nap.

I couldn't resist: I took out a piece of paper from my briefcase and proceeded to write out his confession to theft at the Medical Center. I waited until we landed and after some more of his ribbing and laughing at me that he would "never tell me anything and would never make a confession to anything." As I was getting my bag down from the overhead I said, Doc it was nice flying with you and here's an interesting read. I then handed him a folded piece of paper. With that, the doctor's face turned as white as the paper.

His statement read something like:

My name is Dr. XX,

I am a physician at an area Houston Medical Center for approximately 10 years.

I have caused loss to the medical center and broke hospital policy between my date of hire and present by taking scrubs, medicine and other things from the hospital.

I know this is stealing and I am willing to pay it back if asked. I am aware of others stealing also. Doctors and nurses on the third shift because no one is around and security is usually sleeping.

This statement is the truth.

Signed Dr. XX/Date

If this had been an actual forensic interview, he just confessed his license away, his job, possible jail and restitution and the embarrassment of it all to family, friends and coworkers, not to forget, to himself.

If interview and interrogation are conducted properly and skillfully, the suspect won't even realize he/she is giving up valuable information.

Rapport is built with the interviewee to the extent that he or she believes that the interviewer is the only person on earth that believes and understands them and what they have done. I have been asked out by suspects, after the confession was obtained, for everything from drinks; to dinner; to prayer: to even having sex.

I have <u>never</u> taken any suspect/interviewee up on any offer.

For example:

During WWII the Third Reich's master interrogator for the Luftwaffe, Hanns Joachim Scharff was so skilled, that POW's being interrogated never realized they were giving up valuable information. After the war, the US Air Force invited him to give speeches to military audiences. He would have reunions with former POW's that he interrogated who had stated how nice a guy he was.

Another example of a nice guy interrogator is FBI Special Agent George Piro who interrogated Saddam Hussein. Saddam liked him so much that he gave George his watch, which is on display at FBI Headquarters, and is now a part of FBI history.

Story Time:

At a client's roofing company, while my suspect was writing his confession statement he stopped writing, looked up and said to me:

"You know I just got out of Attica?" I said yes, I do. He said, "I don't know why I am writing this? You're a nice guy." I said, thank you, keep writing. Now, I am no Hanns Scharff, but for an interrogator that was a real compliment.

Summary of Key Points

✔ The difference between a Forensic Accountant and
a Forensic Fraud Examiner
  • When you get it wrong it drives John crazy!
  • Remember "For court" The Forensic Accountant does just
    that, the accounting testimony for court, The Forensic
    Fraud Examiner basically does everything else and then some
  • Not to be confused with a Private Investigator

✔ The IAS process
  • Make clear:
    ○ If you're thinking of stealing, Don't
    ○ If you are, Stop
    ○ If you continue, we will find you

✔ Why people confess
  • All honest people are basically raised the same: To Be Honest
  • A skilled and trained specialist will obtain the confession
    without disrupting the business

Notes or Questions for John

What is the difference between
a Forensic Accountant and a Forensic Fraud Examiner?

John A. Capizzi, CFE, FACFE, DABFE, CHS-3

"If you don't hire John to assist with fraud, theft, embezzlement or related issue, you are working with the second team, make sure you use the first team and don't take any chances. He is worth it."

Michael D Ryan, President and CEO Innovative Financing Solutions

3. SAVING A DIME

Saving a Dime vs Gaining Legal Fees, Workers Comp Claims, Losing Your Credibility

Before becoming my client, most companies typically try to fix their internal problem on their own in order to save a dime. This is understandable, since the company experienced a disruption to business or loss of business due to theft, a lawsuit, etc., etc.

What actually happens is that the company telegraphs to dishonest employees how much the company actually doesn't know, who did what or worse, teaches dishonest employees how to lie, develop alibis, alert co-conspirators, destroy evidence, run or get legal counsel adding more to your loss and expenses.

Let me explain.

Depending on the incident, the interviewer might be the interviewee's direct supervisor, a higher up on the chain of command supervisor, a Human Resource representative, Union representative or even the business owner directly.

The problem is to an untrained interviewer, physical and verbal clues indicative of truth and deception can be missed strengthening a dishonest employee to stick with his/her non-truthful story. We expect everyone to initially lie to us. Especially if the police are notified because now the dishonest employee has the perception that they beat the police when in fact, the officer was only gathering information for a police report to pass onto detectives to investigate if they even take the case.

When a company's representatives attempt to handle a situation that they are not trained for, it can become costly by opening the company up to unforeseen potential labor law violations, false imprisonment allegations, emotional distress allegations, equipment costs and ridicule by staffing. All when the company's intent was to save a dime and cut costs on the investigation.

Example:

A friend of mine, CEO, and client that I have handled internal problems for years had a theft occur in his warehouse. Instead of calling me like he always had in the past, he attempted to handle the situation himself.

He spent a lot of money putting in a CCTV hidden camera system and hours of labor doing the in-house installation. Guess what? The system fell out of the ceiling, all to the hysterical delight of his warehouse staffing! Yes, knowing him it is funny even typing this story.

The day he called me, I went to his office as we were going to lunch after our meeting. He was behind his desk pacing back and forth, ranting about what had happened. I didn't say a word. This went on for some time then he stopped pacing, turned to me shouting: "Well, Say it. Say it. Damn it. Say it!!!!" I replied, Say what? He stared at me for what seemed like minutes, veins popping out of his forehead, then yelled:

"I F****d Up!! I F****d Up!! Are you happy now, that I said it!???" I did all I could not to bust out laughing but he probably would have killed me as he is 6 foot plus. I calmly replied: Are you finished? He yelled his not so calm response, "Yes, fix this damn mess and I don't want to hear it from you!! Let's go to lunch." He then walked out of his office leaving me sitting there.

Funny but true story. The *not* funny part, he had exposed his own company to potential labor law issues, potential workers comp if the system fell on someone's head and someone got hurt, etc., etc., not to forget his credibility.

Did I fix my friend and client's mess? Yes, I was able to get a written, signed, confession from three warehousemen. However, it took longer, as I had to undo everything he did *To Save A Dime*.

<u>Summary of Key Points</u>

✔ Saving a dime
  • Trying to save a dime and not calling IAS can cost you
    more than just money in the end

✔ Gaining legal fees
  • Because you are not an expert at law, or Forensic interviewing,
    trying to handle Fraud and EPL issues on your own,
    can cause you to incur legal fees to protect yourself from
    mistakes made

✔ Workers Comp
  • If you approach the situation the wrong way you could be
    sued for anything from physical harm (cameras falling on
    workers' heads) to Emotional Distress, Pain and Suffering
    on questioning parties involved or suspected, or worse

✔ Losing your credibility
  • If you do any of the above and are not successful in exposing
    the Fraud or EPL, you now put yourself legally and financially
    at risk, as well as, lose your credibility for failing to succeed

Notes or Questions for John

What will you save by calling IAS?

John A. Capizzi, CFE, FACFE, DABFE, CHS-3

"Over the years, he has managed to obtain signed, lawful confessions from dozens of employees, as well as, restitution agreements resulting in the return of thousands of dollars in stolen money."

Lisa Berg, Esq., Partner, Stearns, Weaver, Miller, Weissler, Alhadeff & Sitterson, PA

4. BEFORE A COMPANY BECOMES A CLIENT:

Typically, before a company becomes a client they will reach out to three sources; the police, their accountant, and/or their attorney. Let's talk about each entity.

<u>Police</u>
On a scale of 1 to 10, Internal Theft is the last thing police respond to for several reasons.

The first reason is that your problem is not their priority.

Their first response is to an Officer Needs Assistance call, followed by, for lack of a better description more glamorous calls: Homicide, Armed Robbery, Rape and so on. One step up from Internal Theft in police response is Shoplifting.

Police response to you:
"We are too busy." I can see you nodding your head in agreement!!!

To a degree, police are "Too busy" with violent crimes as you see and hear in daily news reports. Now, let's talk about why you get this response.

To be blunt, there is nothing glamorous about internal theft and fraud. In fact, investigating it can be time consuming, tedious, confusing, even boring.

Trying to figure out a cybercrime and theft of intellectual property, theft of cash from a POS (point of sale system, i.e. cash register), even freight off the loading dock, or a missing night bank deposit can be very boring versus a homicide and smoking gun…. I ask you, which case would you want to pursue if you were in law enforcement?!

Another reason is, the lack of training in this type of case work. However, the biggest reason law enforcement pushes away from internal theft is that, promotions come with solved cases!!

Additionally, the police, if they get involved, may put the time in investigating, then a State Attorney or DA doesn't want to take the case.

I once had an internal fraud case and after a lot of investigative effort on my part with a signed confession and a big blunder by law enforcement, the suspect (with no family) boarded a plane out of country and disappeared forever.

Let me explain this one.

The detective, with an I don't care attitude and minimum training, instead of going to the suspect, called the suspect on the phone, telling him to come into the station.

Well, the suspect did what any self-respecting suspect would do. He boarded a plane to get out of Dodge!!

Needless to say, the detective had a lot of explaining to his Chief as my client was very prominent in the community.

In another case, just as the arrest warrant was being signed, the suspect died. Talk about frustrated detectives!

Accountant

Accountants don't really want to get involved with fraud and internal theft because they are thinking the L word, Liability, and You, my fellow business owners coming at them saying, "I have been paying you all year, why didn't you prevent this"? They are not trained to identify and to prevent it.

Attorney

Internal Theft/Fraud Examination is not taught in Law School. Attorneys, now-a-days need to stay aloof from the investigative process in order to effectively handle the legal matter at hand.

Your Company Integrity, Employees, Physical Structure:

At this point you are probably thinking about the integrity of your own company, employees and the physical structure and on whether it promotes internal problems.

Allow me to pose a couple of questions for you to think about:

- Do you have Loss Prevention measures in place to prevent Fraud and Liability in your business?

- What do you do if you have or suspect a dishonest employee?

- When was the last time that you addressed fraud and liability in your workplace?

<u>Summary of Key Points</u>

✔ Why not the Police?
  • Not as important or as glamorous as say a homicide or smoking gun cases.
  • Promotions happen with solved cases
  • Most importantly, lack of time to investigate
  • and minimum specialized training to solve these types of cases successfully

✔ Why not an Accountant?
  • They do not like to get involved in potential Liability related cases
  • They fear the backlash of blame for not preventing

✔ Why not an Attorney?
  • They are not taught the investigation process and necessity to be aloof from the investigative process

✔ Integrity
  • Questions to consider whether your company promotes or deters wrongdoing

Notes or Questions for John

Who did you think to call?
Hint, answer should be: IAS

"He has always been invaluable in assisting clients detect and close loopholes that help avoid losses from occurring."

Diane Geller, Esq., Partner, Fox Rothschild, LLP.

5. RED FLAGS OF FRAUD
AND CORRECTIVE ACTION

I once analyzed my own files to see if there was a common denominator on why my clients (global) called me. I discovered the following and ask you to assess your business by office, department, division, entirely.

After you review the following "Red Flags" and if you answer Yes, when assessing your business, or answer with a Maybe, (a maybe counts as a Yes), then you have an internal problem in play or one about to happen which you need to address immediately and take corrective action:

23 Red Flags of Fraud in Your Business.
What to Look for:

IAS provides you with the best solutions in detecting fraud and embezzlement. Here is what you can do. Be on the lookout for these telltale signs:

Remember all fraud no matter what the industry are discovered 2 ways only:

1) Accidentally stumbling onto it; or

2) Identified by a disgruntled employee/other tip off

Paying attention to the Red Flags will help you prevent something from happening.

1. An employee under financial pressure.

Financial pressures can include things such as not being able to pay the household bills such as rent, phone, utilities, etc. Indicators include calls to the office from creditors and warnings of utility shutoffs, repossession, credit card companies, garnishments. Other indicators include medical bills, gambling debts, and frequent complaints about losing bets, pools, casino games, etc.

Social expenses: Struggling to keep up with the social network, such as being expected to go out to pricey parties, clubs, events and even charity events with friends.

It can also be as simple as complaints that they need tires for the car and can't afford them or can't afford buying Christmas presents for family and friends during the holidays.

An individual's financial pressures can be as varied as snowflakes in a blizzard.

Example:

I once had a case at a bank in Miami where the teller line funds were found to be consistently short and bank authorities could not determine the cause. In cases like this, I like to observe employees to see their lifestyle. One teller stood out from the rest. She was a very pretty, young twenty something. She would arrive at work driving a BMW or dropped off in a Maserati. She always was impeccably dressed, wearing expensive jewelry and perfume.

One day the investigator/bachelor in me complimented her on the scent of her perfume. I asked where can it be purchased with her reply, "only in France." The investigator in me checked with Human Resources (HR) to inquire on her salary. Lifestyle surely did not match salary. Further, the investigator John always builds rapport with potential interviewee/ suspects by establishing a cordial dialogue.

You are probably saying, Ahh he's got his man and in this case, woman. Right? Semi wrong! Never assume anything. During her interview she stated she was dating a wealthy stock broker and he paid for her "things." She further admitted to taking the money from the bank to pay for expenses to get her family to the USA from Cuba and didn't want to ask her boyfriend to have to pay for this expense.

2. An employee with personality changes.

Anything can trigger this. Stress at home, to being passed over for a promotion, raise or bonus. The once smiling, joking, a pleasure to work with employee is now tense and a nightmare to be around. They are now jumpy, suspicious and complain a lot.

3. An employee demonstrating poor money management.

This could be spending more than they make for a house, car, boat, or buying things not for themselves but for others.

Example:

I had a case involving a funeral home director, located in a poor economic area of the country, who had a full membership at an exclusive private country club. I discovered this when he took me and two client company auditors to lunch. His intent was to distract the auditors from their data gathering. They enjoyed lunch, but I found it to be a tough chew, inquiring with the Club the cost of membership, and then compared the cost to his salary that I found in his HR file.

In another case at a hospital, nurses (RNs) were stealing flu shot cash payments. One RN was taking money to buy expensive gifts for her husband in an attempt to buy him back after he announced he was leaving her.

Or, the case of the CFO who was well known by name at local strip clubs, spending thousands at a time, of course stolen from the company he worked for.

4. An employee living beyond their means.

As noted in Red Flag #1, living beyond one's means can include driving a car beyond their salary range, buying clothes, perfume and jewelry out of their affordable price range vs such things being gifted to them.

5. An employee with outside business interests.

This could be something like working side jobs while on the company payroll clock.

For Example:

The secretary selling Avon or other products from her desk.

I had a case where the company CPA (with a null and void CPA Certificate) was identified and admitted in interview that he was fraudulently signing CPA to company documents and running a "Bookie operation from his office."

Or, the case where the employee/suspect was running a printing company, (his) business after hours, weekends and holidays from the (printing company he was working for.) He wasn't on the clock but he used his employer's equipment, supplies and electricity.

6. Poor Company Controls.

Internal controls are things such as policies and procedures, alarms, CCTV, loss prevention audits and surprise audits to name a few. Not having measures like these in place, means there is no way to prevent or detect if fraud is present, thereby creating a tempting environment for the dishonest employee.

Example:

I was retained by an insurance group to determine the theft of confidential company information and the passing of it to a competitor.

In a 22 page confession, the company president admitted to theft of the confidential information, $50,000 cash theft (which the company was unaware of), bank fraud, check fraud, forgery and attempted arson of another executive's house. When I asked him why he did it, he looked me right in the eye and said: "Because I could."

Another example:

At a trucking logistics company, while I was touring one of its 100,000 sq. ft. distribution facilities with its very proud president, I identified that there was no key control on a Customs Cage built to secure materials waiting clearance from Customs. In addition, a $250,000 new CCTV investment was already defeated by the positioning of the CCTV monitors.

7. Too much control by a single employee.

Too much or total control is when everything from computer passwords, files, accounts payable/receivable, bank accounts, statements, inventory, physical controls, etc. are all in one employee's hands. Without this employee, the company cannot function, payroll can't be processed, bills cannot be paid and the basic of daily operations cannot be accomplished. Comments by an employee about this control such as "this company can't function without me" is a serious Red Flag that there is too much control in one employee.

Case Example:

A client out of Delaware, entrusted all operations to the office manager, a long-time employee and friend of the owner. She wrote checks, received bank statements and made deposits. The owner brought in new business but couldn't pay the monthly bills.

It was identified that she was stealing from the company. In addition to the typical ways of stealing by way of her position, here is one more: The company's fleet of trucks were financed by GMAC. So was her car, her husband's car and two son's vehicles. She simply wrote the checks, brought the checks to the owner for signature, usually when he was distracted on the phone and didn't notice that he signed more checks than vehicles in his fleet. The owner was completely unaware until he read it in her written confession.

8. Lax Management.

This happens when management does not perform basic due diligence Loss Prevention, as well as, not holding personnel accountable for their actions or mistakes in accordance with established policy and procedures, or just do not implement policy and procedures at all.

9. Failure to pre-screen employees, to include checking references.

This includes local and national background checks, drug tests and calling to verify references and employment history.

National background checks (preferred) are necessary because if you only check the state you are located in or where your employee lives, you may miss identifying a prior problem that occurred in another state, prior to your potential employee winding up in your HR or Loss Prevention office.

Case Example:

A large retail client had two locations less than two miles from each other. As I was waiting for my interviewee to come through the door,

I was thinking that the name seems familiar, but I just could not place it. The familiar knock-knock came at the door and in walked a lady whose confession I had taken the year before from the sister store. We looked at each other, I said to her, you know the drill and handed her my standard statement document, she sat and wrote her confession – Again.

On her application, she had listed the sister store that I caught her in the year before! If the manager had picked up the phone and called the sister store, the other manager could have identified her as being terminated for theft, and his store would not have taken a loss. Remember, this is the same company!

10. Records altered, missing or destroyed.

Receipts for reimbursement, bank statements both deposit and withdrawal, expense reports, inventory for stock or office supplies etc., reprinted, whited out, or unable to be found.

Case Example:

I once had a case involving a property management company whose maintenance man would purchase materials for repairs at the local hardware store. If he needed a few nails he would purchase a keg of nails, use the few needed for the repair then return the keg for a refund while splitting the refund money with his cousin, the cashier. No one at the property management company was aware until it came out in his signed confession. Refund receipts were thrown away. Also, as noted in Red Flag #7. (Too much control in a single employee.)

11. Chronic Shortages.

To include inventory, fuel, supplies and petty cash, etc. coming up short as well as being used faster than normal.

Case Example:

During a monthly IAS field Loss Prevention Audit for a construction client, while checking assigned company vehicles for contraband and damage, I came across three vehicles with a three foot length of surgical hose draped over the steering column. On the third discovery, I applied the sniff test. Yep, you got it, the drivers were siphoning fuel. I went to the owner and asked if he had a fuel usage problem.

At first, he said no, but then said, "They were looking into it." I named the three drivers and his response was: "That it can't be, one of those guys is my brother-in-law!!" I replied this is the cause of your high fuel usage. The owner said "John, Go do your thing" and in a couple of hours I had, in hand, three signed confessions with all three saying they were fueling their personal cars.

How would you like to have spent Thanksgiving Dinner that year at his house?!

12. Customer or supplier complaints about shortages, discrepancies, late payments.

Case Example:

A classic means of taking cash is by "aging" (stealing payments then making payment on those accounts from newer "less aged" accounts) from a supplier payment list. Pay attention to incoming complaints by suppliers and vendors for late payments.

13. Signatures on records appear to be forgeries.

Case Example:

An import/export purchasing client out of the Dominican Republic suffered a $15 million-dollar loss by the company CFO forging her husband's (owner) signature. The money was spent on her boyfriend, by gambling and purchasing property. She also put in her written statement that she never divorced her first husband!

Note: If you use a signature stamp, I highly recommend you smash it immediately! It may save you time, but it only tempts an employee to turn dishonest.

14. Employee drug and alcohol abuse.

Any addiction can be costly. Both monetarily where the employee needs money to pay for their addiction as well as inventory depending on the industry; for example, pharmaceutical, medical, or bar and restaurant businesses, etc. where the employee steals inventory (drugs, alcohol) in addition to money to fuel their addiction.

15. Employee gambling problems.

Case Example:

I had a case where the CFO embezzled over $200,000 over a 6 month period gambling at the track and Atlantic City Casino tables.

In his written confession he stated that he "did it because it helped him relax, which helped him do his job better." Unbelievable and yes there is nothing I haven't heard!

16. Employee gives inadequate answers when questioned about missing property, supplies or funds.

An example of inadequate answers would be:
- ✔ Answering your question with a question;
- ✔ Giving you an alibi before even being asked anything;
- ✔ Replies like: "Honest to God;" "On my dead grandmother;" "To tell you the truth."

17. An overwhelming desire for personal gain

I typically see this involving executive management to fuel egos.

Case Example:

I had a case involving a top regional salesman who stole company inventory for resale to the company's clients at a lower price. He would tell his sales clients that he could get what they needed for less, for a nominal service charge for his efforts. When he was identified through the IAS process, he stated in his written confession that he "basically wanted to enjoy the good life like the owner of the company." It was also noted that while developing his profile that this salesman had actually started to mimic the owner's behavior in dress and mannerisms.

18. Close associations with customers or competitors

This is usually an indicator to kickbacks and bribes. Pay close attention to employees frequently hanging out with customers and vendors beyond the course of normal business for example: golfing, fishing trips, shows, wining and dining, plane trips with upgrades, etc...

Corrective action would be written Policy and Procedures along with random interviews of management and staff. I have found that once the employee understands the reasoning behind a loss control procedure, it is easily adapted vs just another hindrance imposed by executive management. I can help.

19. Feeling their pay was not commensurate with responsibility.

This I have found is usually preceded by an employee (management or staff) who has progressively become disruptive, requiring reprimands or other disciplinary action, a drop in work performance, or being disgruntled with comments like "this company can't run without me" and the like.

20. A wheeler dealer attitude.

Case Example:

A Far East client company had a young, intimidating and very controlling executive manager set up his own company out of the country with stolen materials from the company he was employed by. He simply would ship materials directly from the employing company's warehouse to his out-of-country warehouse. He was so intimidating that no one questioned him.

21. A strong desire to beat the system.

This is the employee who always wants to take a short cut as opposed to doing the job right the first time. You can pick him or her out of the crowd. They are usually the one that when you catch them doing something wrong they always have a ready answer for you vs admitting straight out they were wrong or made an error.

22. Undue family or peer pressure.

This can be an overwhelming power on an employee to cause you loss. Be cognizant of your employees whether it's a kid at your franchise prepping fries or some other employee. Be cognizant and get to know your employees. Know their concerns, complaints and worries.

23. Not enough recognition for job performance.

Recognizing this could turn an employee from being a loss control potential problem to a valuable asset to your company. A little praise can often go a very long way in making your employee feel appreciated and recognized.

Case Example:

During one of my monthly Loss Prevention visits to my client's warehouse, I recommended to executive management that we recognize a warehouseman by putting him in a different color company shirt (Blue). The tactic was two-fold: internally, it made him stand out on the shipping/receiving dock; externally, it gave the impression to outsiders who might be watching the operation, of a security patrol on the property.

(The industrial complex had been experiencing break-ins to parked truck trailers.) Why a Blue shirt you might ask? Blue is typically associated with security.

I am sure your experiences and thoughts can add to the list of Red Flags. You have a responsibility to yourself and company to pay close attention to these signs and investigate. And remember:

IAS can help.

What is corrective action?

If you have policies and procedures in place, tweak them wherever you are saying Yes or Maybe to one of the Red Flags of Fraud.

IAS can help.

Loss Prevention Training and Education of employees.

IAS can help.

Random Loss Prevention Interviews of Management and Staff.

IAS can help.

<u>Summary of Key Points</u>

✔ 2 ways Fraud is discovered
  • By accident
  • Disgruntled employees/other informs

✔ 23 Red Flags of Fraud
  • Never put too much control in one employee
  • Be aware of what they are communicating
  • Be aware of their actions and demeanor
  • Be aware of surrounding communication and feedback from other employees or customers
  • Show appreciation to avoid bitter backlash

✔ Corrective Action
  • Tweak policies and procedures
  • Loss Prevention training
  • Random Loss Prevention audits and interviews

Notes or Questions for John

What Red Flags have you seen?

John A. Capizzi, CFE, FACFE, DABFE, CHS-3

"John has been able to obtain the conclusive evidence along with confessions that resolve the matter."

Charles Caulkins, Esq., Managing Partner, Fisher and Phillips

6. CONTACTING IAS FOR HELP

Frequently I am told by business owners and executives, "We are doing good, no need for your services, everything is good I/we have staffing that have been with us for a long time and they are like family."

Let me ask you a question, Do you go to your doctor for follow-up visits, annual checkups, etc.? Yes. Do you take your car in for a tune up, annual inspection? Yes. Well, what about *your* company. Your company is *you* right? Yes.

Something to think about. An FBI stat profile of an embezzler: white, female, with the company 5-10 years, always on the job, willing to pitch in anytime with a smile on her face!!

Grandpop Capizzi was right, "Beware of the guy coming at you smiling!!"

The best scenario for you, when dealing with internal theft, is that you have only one dishonest employee. The worst scenario is that you have several employees all independently stealing from you.

Case Example:

A client based in Massachusetts with a woman's retail operation in El Paso, Texas sent me there less than two weeks before Christmas. I took confession statements from the Store Manager, Store Assistant Manager and six Sales Associates all independently stealing without the other knowing.

When I called the CFO, who was at the Corporate Christmas party he asked me, "How is it going?" I replied that I had signed confessions from all management and staff. He was silent. His next question was: "Do you know how to work a register?" He then said he needed me to stay there until he could get Regional and District personnel there as he could not close the store, located in a mall, two weeks before Christmas.

He then said: "I need you to act Corporate." I replied, What does that mean? He said, "walk around the store, be pompous and point a lot."

I had asked the Store Manager and Assistant Manager if they had any stolen merchandise at home or elsewhere. They replied that they did. I asked them to return the merchandise and they did, rolling rack after rolling rack. They had even stolen the rolling racks from the store! I spent the night tagging each item as evidence with Regional and District management. We didn't walk out of the store until sunrise the next morning. When the "Ladies" appeared in court, the Judge commented on how impeccably dressed they were. Do they know they admitted in court that they were wearing stolen dresses!!

As I said before, there is nothing I haven't heard.

Initial Contact with IAS and What to Expect:

Questions asked to you when you call IAS

Did you discover the problem or did someone inform you?

I ask this because knowing how the problem was discovered will help formulate the forensic examination.

Remember, as previously noted, all fraud is identified two ways only. I repeat: Either by accident/stumbled onto it, or a disgruntled person who tips off the activity sometimes as a diversion.

The person who is informing you of the problem just might be the problem and is trying to cover his/her trail by being able to later say, "I am the one that brought it to the attention of the company." They might be bringing the situation forward because they have a perception (in their head), right or wrong, that they were found out and are now presenting a diversion!

My next question, is to ask the prospective client, Has anyone been interviewed?

If Yes, By Whom and What questions were asked?

Followed by, To the best of your knowledge and recollection, What was the immediate response to the question? The exact response.

I will also ask the client if they want to prosecute or seek restitution should a confession be obtained.

If the client wants to prosecute, I personally take the case to the Economic Crime Detectives in whatever jurisdiction we are in and present the case to them. I then introduce myself and my professional background to the possible future investigating detectives, informing them of my objective of obtaining a signed confession.

They are informed that they are being briefed in the event I don't get a confession; they will be up to speed on the facts of the case. Typically, as a professional courtesy, having had a stint in law enforcement, I can get them to keep the case out of the news for large dollar loss cases, which is always an added value to my client and protects company confidentiality.

Economic Crime Detectives that I have worked with in the past are happy to hear from me asking me, "Is this case like the last?" Remember, promotions frequently come with solved cases and a **(signed confession)** by the man/woman who did it **(is the best piece of real evidence you can get.)**

Note: It is always best to have this in hand prior to police involvement.

The client is then asked to limit and contain communication about the case to a very trusted few.

I ask that the client discreetly stop any actions being taken and we will then schedule a meeting to review the facts of the case and areas of concern.

Sometimes a client will have internal legal counsel and external legal counsel. This can become very cumbersome in putting together and coordinating a successful fraud examination. Egos need to be left in the office.

When it comes time to sit down with the "suspect," it is not the same as conducting an interview via deposition or cross-examination in the safety of one's office or court room.

I have come to really appreciate those attorneys that I have worked with across the country and who know and understand the IAS process, especially when I get a new case and work with attorneys who are new to my process.

I once had a CFO that I knew from a network group that we both belonged to for a long time call me for a case involving the theft of laptop computers from the office work spaces.

I submitted my very "vanilla" engagement agreement. However, I started the preliminary theft examination since the CFO and I were friends and we knew each other for a very long time.

The engagement agreement went back and forth with edit on top of edit (of non-consequential points) by the legal department and then the examination was halted by General Counsel. All the while, more and more laptops were still being stolen from the offices.

The CFO got so frustrated with the company legal department that he paid me for the hours exerted, thanked me profusely, then resigned from the company out of frustration.

Last I heard, the laptops continued to disappear with who knows what else!

Story time again-

An example of Stumbling onto an Internal Problem:

I had a case come to me in the usual manner. An employee in a doctor's office discovered missing money when the Practice Administrator called in sick. She informed the doctor, who then called his attorney (an attorney that I have worked with for well over 28 years) and referred him to me.

The doctor stated his staff identified $1,500.00 missing and he wanted me to handle the case per his attorney's advice. The next thing I knew I was on a plane flying to his location. It was disclosed that the doctor had offices in five locations and the office administrator was in charge of all locations.

Review of the evidence that he had gathered revealed that his losses were approximately $750 provable.

The doctor was asked if he wanted to prosecute and his reply was "absolutely." He was informed that I would be in touch with the local economic crime detectives in his city.

I gave the doctor an assignment of things to look for in each of his other offices in an attempt to determine additional losses not discovered. The doctor agreed to look further into the matter.

In approximately a week and a half my phone rang and it was the good doctor stating that he wasn't looking at anything else in his offices and that he wanted me back to remove the Practice Administrator from her position.

I told him that I highly recommend that he finishes his assignment so that we can determine more realistically what his losses actually are.

He was adamant in stating that he wasn't doing anything else and to just get back and remove her from her position. I notified his attorney and informed her that the doctor was not following my advice and that I thought there might be more losses yet to be discovered. She readily agreed to contact the doctor and advised him to follow my instructions.

He was adamant with her also that he just wanted me back to get her out of his office.

I was on another plane to his location.

Now note, with two flights to his location the cost for airfare well exceeded the $750 identified provable losses.

On arrival, I again advised the doctor against proceeding with the interview of the Practice Administrator without doing the additional fieldwork to determine actual losses. He stated, "I don't care, just remove the Practice Administrator from my office."

I proceeded with the interview and got a $50,000 confession in writing. While she was writing her statement, I left her alone to advise the doctor of the situation.

Now remember, everything I do on scene follows a protocol and is choreographed.

To Explain:

I leave my suspect in an open unlocked office while writing their statement and make sure everyone else in the office sees me, so that if I had to testify in court I can say, I left the suspect alone in an unlocked open office while the suspect continued writing their statement.

I also use this time to advise my client. What I am advising the client, is what is being said in the confession, as well as, how I want them to behave when the written confession is finished and I bring them into the office.

Note: The confession is actually three confessions in one.
- First, verbal to me.
- Second, in writing by the suspect.
- Third, verbal again with the client witnessing.

I will tell the client that when he/she comes into the office he/she is to remain calm, sincere, polite and thank the suspect for their cooperation when finished. I will show them where to sign/date as witness on the statement form. When finished, we will then escort the suspect out of the office.

The reason for this instruction is because the suspect will undoubtedly get an attorney of her own and when he asks her how did she leave the office, I don't want her to say the auditor had to pry the owner's hands from around her throat. Rather, I want her to say the owner was polite and thanked her for her cooperation.

Now back to the story:

I told the doctor she was writing her statement and has admitted to stealing $50,000. I again asked him if he still wanted to prosecute and he replied adamantly, "Yes!" As already stated, I advised him how I wanted him to behave when I brought him into the office. I then returned to the interview office with the suspect.

When she concluded her written statement, I then went to bring in the doctor. He stated to me, there is a change in plans as he had spoken to his wife and "they did not want to put her in prison." He just wanted his money back. I told him that was not a problem and the procedure will be the same as far as his signing and witnessing the statement and reminded him of his controlled behavior.

I further told him that he could make an offer for restitution and that it had to come from him to her as I do not make any threats, promises or offers to the suspect. I provided him with a blank Promissory Note with an option for payment in full or payment in installments and instructed him to present this to her after she admitted again, and he signed the statement witnessing her confession.

All went as usual in my cases. The doctor informed her that he did not want to put her in prison and he just wanted his money back and presented her with the Promissory Note. She readily agreed to pay him back. I injected one thing prior to my departure informing her that when she paid the doctor that she pay him in cash or a bank draft. I, as a Forensic Fraud Examiner, did not want her to take the opportunity to possibly write him a fraudulent check.

I then thanked both the doctor and my suspect and departed for the airport. On my way to the airport, as a professional courtesy, I called the economic crime detectives that I had met less than two weeks prior and informed them of the confession and that criminal action was off the table because the doctor elected for restitution.

The detectives informed me that during those two weeks they had run her through the NCIC (National Crime Information Center) Database and got a hit that she was a convicted embezzler. They further did a background and determined that she had a house, a couple cars and a boat.

Note: No way could she afford this on her salary.

Bright and early the next morning, my cell phone rang with the caller shouting "John, it's Dave, it's Dave!" I replied, Dave who? He replied "Dr. XX!" The good doctor called to thank me because she came in that morning carrying a shopping bag with $50,000 in cash.

I congratulated him and informed him that it was his money.

I further informed him what the detectives had told me on my way to the airport. I informed him that if he had listened to me, the confession would probably be much higher and that she would have had an express ticket to the Gray Bar Motel (that's Jail) and that the court very well might have ordered restitution through her estate.

He asked if anything could be done, and I said no - he sealed the deal by accepting the money.

On his behalf, I have to say, it would be difficult for anybody to refuse a shopping bag with $50,000 in cash!!

Our suspect knew that if she could get a restitution offer and close the deal with full payment she would escape prison.

What she apparently did, was save a substantial amount of money in the event that she got caught; she knew she could buy her way out.

What happened in her interview with me was when I did not blink at her $50,000 confession she knew I had no idea how much she actually had taken. If the doctor had listened to me when she admitted $50,000 and he had done his assigned homework, I would've told her to rethink her admission and the dollars would have gone up. End of story.

Let's take a minute to discuss what actually happened here.

The typical business owner is embarrassed to admit that his staff beat him in protocol and stole from him/her.

If you noticed I have a lot of letters after my name CFE, DABFE, FACFE, CHS-3. They are not there for an, "At A Boy John" but are there to make someone ask what do the letters represent, while allowing me an opportunity to talk about what I do.

It opens the door for a potential client to talk to me without feeling embarrassed.

As previously identified, my biggest hurdle is getting people to believe that I will get a confession.

In this case, the doctor's friends gave him bad advice, stating "He was throwing good money after bad, nobody is going to confess, it's an *at-will state* and to just remove her."

The Doctor, I believe, was embarrassed by the situation in front of his friends and his friends hounding him with their so called advice.

I did tell the doctor the next time he is at his Club for lunch, to thank his friends for being so generous with his money.

The doctor is now a believer in me and my process.

Another story:

Example of a Tip-off:

There was a case I had in a southern state involving several auto dealerships.

The enterprising staff utilized out-of-country obituaries obtaining Social Security numbers and American real estate address listings to manipulate the dealership's financing system.

The salesmen and others were making a fortune on sales and commissions to the extent of flaunting their new-found fortune by way of flashing cash, Rolexes and other bling.

It took an angry girlfriend to tip off the scheme because she caught her salesman boyfriend sharing his new fortune with a couple of entertainers at a local strip club.

The identified loss to the dealerships was approximately $42 million, and the scrubbing of the manufacturer's financing system until it could be reworked. The case resulted in twelve federal indictments obtained from the evidence gathered and signed confessions.

How Long will the Fraud Examination Take?

Frankly I don't know.

Clients are almost always in a rush to get the Fraud Examination over as fast as possible.

I always have to remind them that the suspect or suspect(s) had all the time in the world to put their dishonest activities into play and at their leisure.

We, (client and I) need to piece the puzzle together without the puzzle box top to look at. The pieces include determining a start date of incident, determining who is involved, one or several people, gathering evidence, developing interviewee profiles, establishing the client's probable cause statement, background checks if needed, the interviews of employees.

Just to name a few considerations. There are more!

The Client Probable Cause Statement:

When I am retained I will ask the client to provide me with a detailed statement from them, detailing what the situation is, how they discovered the situation, who is allegedly involved, etc., etc...

The purpose of obtaining the client statement is to establish the probable cause of the case should it take the prosecution route. Also, to establish the case for insurance claims and for me to develop my course of action in forming the forensic examination.

I usually get a groan from the client but either way they will have to eventually provide their statement so they should get it out of the way from the start.

I also found over the years that when the client writes/types their statement (in detail), they typically provide many more details of vital importance for a successful outcome to their case than what they initially provide to me in their initial verbal consultation.

It is vital to keep the investigative process contained to a handful of trusted personnel.

We typically have one opportunity to sit with the suspect(s). We need to stay off their radar so we don't alert them to develop alibis, destroy evidence, warn co-conspirators, run, or "lawyer up" as they say in the movies.

The longer we are off their radar, the more time we have to gather evidence that will be presented to them during their interview with documents to be initialed/dated as evidence as a companion to their signed confession.

<u>Summary of Key Points</u>

- ✔ Contacting IAS and what to expect
  - Did you discover the Fraud or did someone else?
  - Who asked the questions and what questions where asked?
  - What was their immediate physical and verbal response?

- ✔ Remember everything is Choreographed
  - From introductions
  - to the open, unlocked office

- ✔ 3 Confessions in one
  - Verbal
  - Written
  - Verbal with witness

- ✔ How long is the process?
  - Depends on:
    - ○ Start date of Fraud
    - ○ Who/How many involved
    - ○ Develop suspect profiles
    - ○ Establish cause AND more

- ✔ Probable Cause Statement
  - A must for prosecution
  - Reveals vital info
  - Just get it done! It helps more than it could ever hurt

<u>Notes or Questions for John</u>

Do you have your answers ready?

*"John has an uncanny talent to ferret out the truth
and is tenacious and relentless in his efforts to protect
his client's interests."*

Mark Skipper, Esq., Principal Skipper Law Group

7. OH CRAP, I ALREADY SPOKE
TO MY EMPLOYEES

What now? and What Can Go Wrong?

My clients know that when things go wrong at their company to: **Stop, Call me and Discuss** all aspects of the situation and any actions that they may have taken.

In order to achieve a successful outcome, I cannot emphasize enough how important it is for me to be involved at the very beginning when the problem is discovered before any actions are taken to correct it.

So what could go wrong?

We already discussed telegraphing which informs the bad employee how much the company doesn't know; who did what and teaching the employee how to lie.

Now in my line of work, I expect and anticipate all to lie to some degree. Yes, all to lie.

My client will lie due to the embarrassing incident itself because his employees got something over on him.

Please remember, I am here to help you. When you call me I need to know everything you know and there is nothing I haven't heard before.

Management will lie because they know that, you the boss, will be questioning them on how /why they let it happen.

The dishonest employee will lie due to fear of jail, restitution, termination, or embarrassment.

You might be saying: "I have a brother-in-law who's a cop and I'll just call him in and he will do the interview of the suspect employee."

Well if he's a sworn police officer, prior to him talking to an employee as a "suspect," he has to by law, inform the employee of the Miranda Warning, as he is acting as a police officer in the performance of his duty and under the color of law.

You know Miranda, "You have the right to remain silent, you have the right to an attorney and anything you say can and will be used against you" etc. etc.

If that employee/suspect says I want to invoke my right to be silent and I want an attorney, the interview must be concluded.

You now have the added expense of having to get an attorney to talk to your suspect's attorney.

Guess what? You are now on the suspect's radar and we discussed what that means.

You might be saying: "I have a sister-in-law who is an attorney or human resource specialist. They can send letters to the suspect demanding whatever it is you need as evidence."

Guess What? You're on the radar and there goes the evidence and suspect(s).

Can I Just Polygraph?:

When I am giving a presentation the question of polygraph testing frequently comes up, so let's discuss this.

Under today's labor laws you better be better than 95% + + sure he or she did whatever you are trying to find out, otherwise, you are going to open yourself up to labor lawsuits.

In addition, The Polygraph Protection Act states that you have to give the person 24 to 48 hours advanced notice and tell them the questions to be asked.

Now, with that said, hope he shows up, shows up without his attorney, doesn't alert co-conspirators and doesn't destroy evidence. On top of this, it costs money and disrupts your business creating a finger pointing atmosphere.

After all this, guess what, you can't use the results in court. That's right: It's *not* admissible.

Now let's discuss the Forensic Interview.

The Forensic Interview
Interview vs Interrogation:

What is a Forensic Interview?

It is a non-threatening, non-accusatory interview utilized to clear an interviewee or to pursue a confession.

This type of interview can be used in fraud cases, HR issues, dealing with vendors and in depositions.

When the verbal confession is obtained, we follow up with the written confession statement which is admissible in court and is the best piece of real evidence.

Basically, this interview process can be utilized anytime you want to know if someone is lying.

There is only one stipulation as I always state in my presentations to corporations, professionals and law enforcement:

- *Never use this on family and friends as there are times that you don't want to know when someone is lying!!*

I had a client whose General Counsel said to me, "you call it an interview, but it's an interrogation."

Do you know the difference?

You better know the difference because sometime, somewhere if you are the one handling internal case work this is going to come up by a savvy defense attorney doing his job trying to make you look stupid while trying to get his client off.

Don't think it is necessary for you to know the difference?

Let's Look at the Stats:

Fraud Stats

I can make this statement because statistically speaking according to the Association of Certified Fraud Examiners, identified fraud in the United States is:

- well over a $900 billion problem;
- with an average company losing 6% of its revenue
- or $9.00 per day per employee
- with 84% of the worst fraud committed by employees, half having been with the company 5 years.

The stats don't include the figures from non-reported fraud or when someone admits $100K and its actually $200K.

So you see, the probability with Fraud Stats this high is that you will be involved with a fraud/ internal problem sometime in your career. Remember:

IAS can help!

Interview

You/We do this all the time all day long. It is simply gathering information. No more. No less.

Interrogation

The Interview becomes an Interrogation when in the mind of the interviewer you go from just gathering information to your intent being to hear the interviewee say: "I did it." It is non-threatening, non- accusatory and structured to extract a confession.

You might see or hear in the press, "Law enforcement interrogate suspect for 24 hours."

That statement is misleading as the Interrogation is the time one is speaking with the suspect. It doesn't count for the time it takes for the suspect to write their statement or go through evidence initialing and dating.

Summary of Key Points

What could go wrong?!

✔ Everyone will lie
- Client- Embarrassment "They got over on me!"
- Management- Ashamed "The Boss thinks I let it happen"
- Dishonest Employee - Fearful, "I don't want to get caught"

✔ If you tell the cops
- Mandatory Miranda warning
    ○ Encourages Silence and Attorney

✔ If you tell an attorney or HR
- They must now reach out to suspect's attorney before contact, now on suspect's radar
- Destruction of evidence; alibis and tip off to co-conspirators

✔ Polygraph
- Needs advance notice and identify questions to be asked
- Time to prepare lies and alert co-conspirators
- Not admissible, i.e. no good in court

✔ Forensic Interview
- Non-Threatening/Non-accusatory
- Clear employee or pursue confession

✔ Interrogation
- The intent of the interviewer is to obtain a confession and hear "I did it"

<u>Notes or Questions for John</u>

What has gone wrong?

John A. Capizzi, CFE, FACFE, DABFE, CHS-3

"I always found him to be professional and to have expertise in internal audit matters.

Don Works, Esq., Principal, Jackson Lewis, P.C.

8. IAS ARRIVAL AT YOUR BUSINESS

The facts and evidence of the case will be re-reviewed with the client and trusted inner staff.

The client's probable cause statement will be re-reviewed with the client and expanded on if needed.

The extent of losses will be identified as accurately as possible.

The time frame to report to your insurance company, so your crime coverage won't be jeopardized, will be determined.

Developing the Interviewee Profile

A profile of the interviewee will be developed identifying what is normal behavior for the interviewee.

I will ask you and inner trusted staff to separately tell me about each interviewee specifically. For example,

Is he/ she moody, belligerent, family oriented, religious, married, single, kids. When identified doing something wrong, do they readily admit to it or do they always have an excuse, as well as, other questions.

I need to develop the profile about the person in order to develop rationales on why they did what they did, and also to distinguish between their normal behavior and deceptive indicators that may be detected during the forensic interview.

All the information that you can provide about the interviewee is vital. What may seem as irrelevant to you may be very important to me.

Example:

A president of a company once made a side comment to me that the interviewee was the only employee that did not come to the company Christmas party. When I brought this up during the interview, my suspect broke down crying and confessed.

Our suspect had an overwhelming sense of guilt because the president/owner of the company had done a lot for the suspect. The owner helped him buy his first house, helped him get an education and basically gave him an opportunity with the company. Our suspect was overcome with guilt.

As you can see from this example, everything is important when we (You and I) talk before the interviews take place.

Interview Room Setting:

I will also ask you to provide a quiet, private room or office to conduct the interviews in.

Office setting preferably:

- ✔ 10' by 10', conventional office;
- ✔ Not too large or too small;
- ✔ Good lighting;
- ✔ Good ventilation;
- ✔ No distractions, No one walking through or interrupting;
- ✔ No phone calls;
- ✔ Table/desk clear of distractions, nothing on it;
- ✔ 2- straight legged chairs: No arms, No wheels (preferred);
- ✔ No pictures or signs that can be a reminder of punishment. For example, a poster stating, "We Prosecute Everyone."

Story time:

I had a case where I and my interviewee were both sitting in chairs that had wheels on the legs. The nervous energy exerted by the interviewee had him rolling away from me with me in hot pursuit during the interview process. It wasn't until he ran out of rolling room that we continued the interview from a stationary position.

Therefore, I highly recommend chairs without wheels. I also recommend that you sit in the same type of chair as your interviewee. In other words, don't sit in a Lazy Boy while your interviewee sits in a hard wood chair. It can be used against you by that savvy defense attorney.

In another case, that savvy defense attorney that I keep mentioning showed up while I was testifying in court. The attorney had earlier asked to see the room where his client was questioned.

On the day, he went to my client's office to view the room, a florescent light bulb was burning out and flickering. Do you know that attorney tried to allege in court that his client was placed under a strobe light!!

In another case, yours truly forgot what I teach in reference to making sure that there are no reminders of punishment in the interview room.

During the interview, every time I mentioned the missing money my suspect would look up and to the right. I eventually got the confession and written statement but it took much longer than it should have based on the preponderance of behavior clues during the interview.

Afterward I looked around the room and noticed on an upper shelf was a picture of the store manager's son. So what, you might say!

Well, the picture was of the manager's son, a uniformed police officer standing in front of an American Flag. Translation: The picture of a police officer, was a reminder of punishment to my suspect. Effect: Anxiety, delaying her confession.

It is always better to do the interview one on one if possible.

For my Catholic readers, I ask you, where would you rather go to Confession, one on one in the Confessional, in the dark, disguising your voice (the priest always knew it was me) or on a kneeler, on the altar in front of everyone who is counting the minutes you're up there!!

There are many other things to consider. For example, an interview with a witness, an interview with a translator. Where do they sit, what do they do during the interview, etc.

Call me to discuss. Remember: I can help.

Can you tape record the Interview/ Interrogation?

Now let's talk about another topic that frequently comes up in my presentations, can you record the interview/interrogation?

Federal statutes say one party consent (You) is no problem.

However, depending on what State you are in some State Statutes require 2 party consent so you will need your interviewee's consent to record.

Sure, it makes it easier for you later on writing your report and relieves the burden of taking accurate notes during the interview or minimizes the possibility of you missing something. However, it will hinder both you and your interviewee because you will be both paying attention to the recorder impeding the flow of information. Or worse, you forget the recorder, it stops, now you have no recording and no notes of the interview.

Or, it might give that old savvy defense attorney some unknown recorded sound like your knee accidentally hitting the table leg, so he can allege "The noise recorded was you striking his client to get an admission." Remember, he will allege anything to get his client off and make you look stupid and unprofessional.

If you insist on recording, I recommend a time/dated video recording.

Start taping before your interviewee walks into the room and stop recording after he/she leaves the room. You still need to get their consent.

Now add in possible stage fright, from both of you, that will hinder the interview process.

This process can also be quite expensive, and if you have to travel to the location for the interview, you will get your work out carrying camera equipment, brief case, evidence and as necessary your luggage. Still want to record?

Post Suspect/ Employee Interviews:

IAS guidance continues even after the last interview and signed confessions are obtained, including dealing with police, restitution, press, insurance, policy and procedures, security measures, loss prevention training and education.

IAS extensive value-added business network referrals can assist you in locating replacement personnel, security, etc.

Monthly industry specific and client specific Loss Prevention/ Risk and Liability audits can be developed, even point scored, if the client has multiple locations further promoting the IAS proactive methodology of:

- ✔ If you are Thinking of causing loss and risk, Don't;
- ✔ If you are causing loss and risk, Stop; and
- ✔ If you Continue you will be Identified.

Some insurance companies may give a reduction in Crime Coverage Premiums due to your company being proactive with monthly IAS visits to (prevent) claims and losses from occurring.

Similar to when you put an alarm on your car or house. What you save in insurance may pay for a continued value-added Loss Control Program.

This value adds up. How much will you save in time, peace of mind, money and stress with an ongoing Loss Prevention Monthly Program?

Find out more at:

www.internalauditservices.com

Text RedFlag to 72727

OR

Call Direct 561-602-0571

<u>Summary of Key Points</u>

✔ Upon Arrival
- Facts/evidence Re-reviewed
- Probable Cause Statement expanded if necessary
- Extent of losses identified
- Insurance Time frame assessed

✔ Developing Profile
- Personality/Mood/Typical reaction to feedback
- What is their Normal behavior?
  - ○ Base for detecting deceptive indicators

✔ Ideal Room Setting
- Not too large or too small
- Good lighting/ventilation
- No distractions/interruptions/or reminders of punishment
- No wheels on chairs or they roll away!

✔ Recording
- Depending on state it may be illegal without their consent
- With consent, causes distraction

✔ What happens when it's over
- We stay with you all the way
  - ○ Talk to Police, Court, Restitution
  - ○ Referrals for replacements
  - ○ Updating Policy & Loss Prevention training

Notes or Questions for John

Are you ready?

Wanted: Employee Thieves

"He is relentless in protecting his client's interest's and a very valuable asset to any company needing to proactively resolve and prevent internal problems."

Muna Issa, Managing Director, Super Clubs Resorts, Kingston, Jamaica

9. IAS ASSISTANCE PROGRAMS

Training Programs are available for your company or organization such as:

Loss Prevention training; Interview and Interrogation Training for Fraud and Liability in the Work Place. This training will enhance your Management, HR, Legal and yourself in interviewing employees and potential employees minimizing potential liabilities to your company.

One-on-one consultation;

Available to you to minimize losses and potential liability to your company that may result should your case not be handled properly and effectively by less trained or non-specialized trained personnel.

Assistance in developing Loss Prevention Controls and Policy and Procedures;

Customized Monthly Loss Control Proactive Audits.

These are custom developed for your operation depending on your industry. The operational audit can also be point scored if you have multiple locations inducing a competitive nature between your location management as no one wants to be low score at your management meetings.

Monthly involvement with your company as an ongoing proactive Loss Control Program as discussed may reduce your Crime Coverage Insurance Premium, similar to putting an alarm on your house or car as a preventive measure to loss control rather than reactive after the fact to a loss.

The Customized Monthly Loss Control Proactive Audits keeps Loss Prevention fresh in the mind of both management and staff personnel, reduces opportunity to cause loss and identifies Loss Prevention vulnerabilities to the company. It also ensures your company employees are functioning in the capacity that *you* think they should be.

Facility Vulnerability Assessment;

Your facility can be assessed to identify vulnerabilities that would promote and induce internal theft and other non-productive activities;

Law enforcement Liaison;

This liaison can enhance your physical security as well as enhance police response to your needs while providing a deterrence to outside criminal influences both on your work force and physical property.

Coming soon on-line video training.

Summary of Key Points

✔ One-on-one consultations
  • Personalized just for you

✔ Developing Loss Prevention
  • Set up Policy and Procedures
  • Conduct Monthly Loss Prevention audits

✔ Vulnerability assessment
  • Where are your flaws, holes and leaks?

✔ Liaison
  • Handle police interaction for less confusion and less stress

✔ Keep an eye out!
  • For online training
  • Seminars and workshops

Find out more at:

www.internalauditservices.com

Text RedFlag to 72727

OR

Call Direct 561-602-0571

<u>Notes or Questions for John</u>

Which service will you use?

John A. Capizzi, CFE, FACFE, DABFE, CHS-3

"I learn from John each time we talk and his counsel is always sound. His unconventional approaches to clever schemes keep him one step ahead of the bad guys who work amongst us."

Paul Donahue, Centerra Group, CEO/ Constellis COO, formerly G4SGS, President &CEO; WSI, COO and CFO.

10. CONCLUSION

I hope you enjoyed my book and stories. You asked for it, you got it. If I can be of assistance please call me direct. I look forward to hearing from you.

I will close with as Detective Lt. Columbo would say: "One More Thing." In this context, One More Story.

Story time:

I was giving a lecture at Florida International University in Miami, Florida. An old friend was there, Dr. Mort Dittenhoffer, coauthor of "Sawyer On Internal Auditing" with Larry Sawyer. This is the textbook for the profession of Internal Audit. This was his class.

It was a real honor to teach in the classroom of the man that wrote the book. I must say, very stressful for me when Mort would stay and listen while I taught my fraud section. This is a man that has forgotten more than I will ever know! Mort would say, "I like your stories." I was glad when he would leave the classroom.

Mort, would have me present to his graduate students when covering Fraud. Some students are current business people, C Level Execs and the like.

Prior to one particular class, I stopped off at the men's room and overheard two students (current CFO's) discussing their "Plan."

One student, asked the other to "cover for him" as he had a hot date on South Beach. He further asked his friend if he "would give him a copy of any notes taken and sign him in so he would get credit" The other student agreed.

My lecture went on with the enthusiasm of the students asking questions. Just prior to class concluding a woman raised her hand and stated to me in a questioning tone: "You must not trust anyone working as a Forensic Fraud Examiner?"

Those that have attended my classes and presentations know I teach by examples.

Keeping with my style of teaching, I continued: "Fraud is everywhere, it is even in this classroom." You could have heard a pin drop! My class turned into an atmosphere like kids sitting around a camp fire listening to a ghost story!!

I described the conversation I heard in the men's room as if it was a criminal act and not just something against school and Dr. Dittenhoffer's policy.

I said, Ladies and Gentlemen *"of the jury"* the facts of the case are as follows:

Two individuals have a conversation plotting, planning and then executing their plan to cover for the other who was cutting my class for a hot date. I suggest that you view this as a *Conspiracy*.

Review of the evidence identified one student signing the other in for my class. This could be considered *Forgery* and *Falsifying Documents*.

Should the "suspect" that cut my class get credit for the class, even though he was not present? I suggest Ladies and Gentlemen of the jury that you deem that *Theft!*

Now, the only question the suspect(s) have to ask themselves is this:

Is this Forensic Fraud Examiner going to turn them in to be executed by Dr. Ditttenhoffer?

I picked up my brief case and said, "Good night, see you next week." As I walked out, I glanced at my "suspect student" and he was white as a perspiring ghost!

I told Mort, but I didn't give up the names. We had a good laugh.

You have to have a sense of humor in this profession of dealing with lies, deceit, emotion and wrongdoing.

I guarantee, those two students/CFO's learned something to take back to the office.

Case closed.

<u>Summary of Key Points</u>

What have you learned?

- ✔ The difference between a:
  - ○ Forensic Accountant &
  - ○ A Forensic Fraud Examiner
  - ○ Not a Private Investigator

- ✔ Where is Fraud
  - • Everywhere; even in graduate school classrooms

- ✔ How to identify Fraud
  - • The 2 ways it is discovered
  - • 23 Red Flags to know you have it

- ✔ The process of IAS
  - • From first Consultation call
  - • To information gathered
  - • To onsite procedures
  - • And types of confessions provided
    - ○ First verbal; Second written; Third verbal with a witness
  - • The power of a skilled Forensic Fraud Examiner

- ✔ What happens when it's over
  - • IAS is there for you all the way
  - • Additional value added
  - • And other prevention measures

Now you know who to call to handle Fraud and Employment Practices Liabilities and who to call to prevent it. So what are you waiting for? **<u>IAS can help, so call today!</u>**

Notes or Questions for John

Are you prepared?

John A. Capizzi, CFE, FACFE, DABFE, CHS-3

Find out more at:

www.internalauditservices.com

Text RedFlag to 72727

OR

Call Direct 561-602-0571

REFERENCES

Association of Certified Fraud Examiners (Stats)

Federal Bureau of Investigation (Stats)

The Interrogator by Raymond S. Toliver, 1997
ISBN 0-7643-0261-2

ABOUT THE AUTHOR

John A. Capizzi (with decades of experience in criminal investigations) is Principal of the firm Internal Audit Services, Inc., Int'l. specializing in fraud examination, and forensic interviewing, risk assessments, risk analysis and loss prevention, throughout the United States and abroad.

Mr. Capizzi is a Certified Fraud Examiner; Board-Certified Forensic Examiner; Fellow, American College of Forensic Examiners; Diplomat, American Board of Forensic Examiners; Certified in Homeland Security, CHS-3. He is a Past Director and a Past President of the South Florida Chapter of the Association of Certified Fraud Examiners and a former member of the Association's Trial Review Board, which investigates violations of the CFE Code of Ethics nationally and internationally.

He is a past member of the Board of Governors and a Past President of the Miami Chapter of the Institute of Internal Auditors. Professional member and national speaker, Society for Human Resource Management (SHRM); listed in the National Registry of Forensic Examiners; Member, The Union League of Philadelphia; a former member of the Palm Beach County Hotel and Motel Association; former member Greater Fort Lauderdale Lodging and Hospitality Association, as well as, a former long-time member of the Executive's Association of Fort Lauderdale, Florida.

Mr. Capizzi has lectured to audiences both foreign and domestic: Senior Auditors of the Auditor General's Office of the People's Republic of China; Canadian Blue Cross and Blue Shield; British government officials of the Turks and Caicos Islands; International Conference on New Developments in Government Financial Management with representatives from El Salvador; Trinidad and Tobago; St. Kitts, W.I.; Federated States of Micronesia; Mauritius; Bahamas; Costa Rica; World Bank- USA; Albania; Antigua; Argentina; Barbados; Bolivia; Brazil; Chile; Columbia; Dominican Republic; Ecuador; Egypt; Uganda; Honduras; Equatorial Guinea; Georgia; Ghana; Guatemala; Greece; Haiti; Indonesia; Lithuania; India; Latvia; Malaysia; Nicaragua; Mexico; Netherlands – Antilles; Pakistan; Panama; Paraguay; Peru; Philippines; Poland; Puerto Rico; Slovenia; Ukraine; Sierra Leone; South Africa; United Kingdom; Uruguay; Venezuela; Vietnam; Zimbabwe; University – graduate level; Corporate; Internal Audit Departments; Professional Organizations; Security; Private Industry and Law Enforcement, Municipal, State and Federal.

Received Appointment United States Naval Academy, Jacksonville University, Jacksonville, Florida, BS degree 1980.

Knighted, Dynastic Order of Savoy, Italy, Order of Saints Maurice and Lazarus, recognized by the Vatican.

Made in the USA
Middletown, DE
01 May 2018